BEAUTIFUL BRUTAL

POEMS ABOUT CATS

AMY MILLER

CYCLONE PRESS

ASHLAND, OREGON

"The Cat Instructs" previously appeared in *Apalachee Review*
and the chapbook *The Stablehand's Report*.

Cover image: Georg Flegel (1566–1638)
*Zitronen in einer Schale, welche auf einer Käseschachtel steht,
ein Korb voller Wal- und Haselnüsse, eine aufgeschnittene Zitrone,
ein Messer, eine Maus, die von einer Walnuss nascht und
eine Katze auf einem Holztisch*

Cyclone Press

🐾

Ashland, Oregon
writers-island.blogspot.com
amymillerediting@gmail.com

Beautiful Brutal: Poems about Cats
Expanded Edition
ISBN 978-0-9839274-4-0
First printing: March 2014

For Melinda

and for Sirina, Gracie, Tara, Salome,
Iniki, Caesar, Buster, Deja, Chloe,
and the Year of Nine Cats

CONTENTS

FLYING CAT

In her dream the cat takes flight,
spreads his paws like wings
and aims and flies.
He is happy, a reckless guest
in the empire of birds,
parting the upper limbs
in the way
of dreams. Death
is shut in another room.
So many could fall tonight—
the cat crossing the sky,
the birds in scatter of panic—
but this is not
how the dream ends.
In the morning, the cat
minds his bowl, the birds
guard their fence. The dream
still plays in her head
as she watches steam rise
off the pouring tea
until it finds the ceiling
and pools as water,
seeing her upside down,
her own feet
holding her
to the floor.

HELLO KITTY

He sees you coming
and flees
like a moon
is about to plow
into his civilized
planet. He might come
when you call,
but it better
be something good:
a toy tossed
like a small felt
cadaver. Otherwise,
food is never bad.
When you arrive home,
hello will do
and maybe a gesture—
an arm swept
to embrace the house
and him in it.
It's fine
to be abstract.
He sees you.
He hears you.
Others have left him
before. He is waiting
to see what kind of hello
you really are.

THE CAT INSTRUCTS

There is no destination.
He plays with a light orange ball
that is all turnabout,
banked off a baseboard,
sideways off his paw,
his tail coming round
like a boom. Ball and cat
and house ignite a universe
of acceleration, tangents struck
at random, every outcome
branched with outcomes of its own,
every turn a life begun,
every pause a brink
before the infinite.

THREE HAIKUS

Hot August evening.
Three cats lie in a circle.
In winter, they fought.

*

The chair is ruined.
Three hundred dollars—ruined!
Still, the cat claws it.

*

In bed, nine a.m.
Three cats pinned against my legs.
The coffee can wait.

NAMING THE KITTEN

You must come around to it,
like your point in a Japanese
conversation. You must find
his shape and line and air.

It should be tall and languorous,
braced with a beam
of balance. It should clothe him
seamlessly as he walks.

Beau is right but wrong,
too quickly spoken, easily
misheard. Nathan is run
with oddly eastern streets.

Before you sleep, you list
the hurricanes, the star-
mad astronomers, every
liquid, Latin shortstop.

Even on the street, your ears
reach down the alleys,
wash over every open mouth,
hoping someone will say it.

CAESAR AT FOUR MONTHS

The shelter smell
still lingers,
factory flea-can,
the despotic clean
of the neuter clinic.

His eyes contain
all the colors
they still could be:
marble green, temple gold,
the blue of turquoise
under water.

He lugs his man-sized
paws around the house,
pads ham-pink, precise
Caucasian baby toes.

Curled in my elbow,
he practices the sleep
of the mighty
when they are young,
before they wander out,
blinking, to their own glory.

CAT WITH A BOUQUET OF ROSES

First, it is change,
crystal vase creasing the fabric
of night, bent space
in a water-bound mirror.
It lures her like a pond
in the salt flat
of the coffee table,
bright pool at the base
of redhead trees,
leaves limp as desire.
One arm in,
she carefully parts the stems
to feel on her black foot
the shudder of that other
element, that not-air,
not-floor. She lifts back
the soaked paw,
tastes it, dips again.
Where this is going
is the other end
of discovery:
the slow tip
of the heavy glass,
the scrape of its skid
as the lip falls down,
sudden gush
of cold, crash
of stems, flowers
beached like soft, fat fish.
She steps along the new shore,
tide creeping
toward a pile of books.

ANIMAL MEDICINE

You look at them
differently now.

The cat, alert on the window sill,
has no eye for horizons.
With legions of limp gophers
and cottonball quail chicks,
she has made you understand this.
You have wiped blood
from her bowl.

The Dalmation, his bent-spring body
a coiled blur in the marsh grass,
his rounded howl the face of joy,
spots the ears of a jackrabbit
and is gone, around the levee
and out of sight.
No one's voice can call him back.
A half mile on,
you find the rabbit's shoulder
hanging like an iceberg
in the slough.

You came to this island
to drink the world,
but the brew is bitter:
nutmeg and brine,
camphor and salt,
the rind of the melon.
Animal medicine.
And you drink.

CATNIP

She no longer visits.
She's lost me
in the bergamot mint, a forest
of green spades and rust stems,
a smell too sharp for her
imperial black nose.

The midnight crush we had,
her purr like hail
on walnut leaves, her sudden,
drunken clutch, the swipe
of teeth raking stem. I died
every night beneath her.

But now, this beast of bergamot,
a garrison of stink
amassed on oiled parapets.
Someone thought me
frail enough to need
an army in the night.

I struggle toward the moon,
waving among tall heads
of green. I send her
scent missives, hear her
hunting crickets, balanced
on beautiful, brutal paws.

BREATH

How nice it must be for the cat,
not knowing where his parents are,
washing his face, not knowing
if they're alive or dead
or living in a dirty house
or long gone back
to God's green garden full
of dragonflies and summer.

How nice it must be
to nod his head down
to the pillow, not thinking
of ruination, not thinking
of taxes or how Dad goes
too often to the dentist—
no insurance for that—
like washing the car
with a comet on the way.

The day is warm. The cat's belly
is full of breakfast and he and I
together pulled all the burrs
from his tail an hour ago, and now
that work is done. Next
he turns to the task at hand:
his sleep, his slow,
miraculous breath.

CAT IN MIRROR

His yellow eyes are trained
on me. He's thrilled
by any shard of light,
the dappled sun his drink,
strong noon heat
enough to fill him whole,
the lamps of night some kind
of lullaby, warming him to sleep.
He never tires of the mirror
leaned on the baseboard,
a window back on his world,
even his own
small face mythic,
inverted, as if
there were one more
of everything,
backward, beckoning
just beyond the glass.

OCTOBER, AFTER RAIN

the cat's cool fur
under my hands
saturated watersilk
wild wind come home

nose
like the tip
drip
off an icicle

sharp scent I wish
I carried
on my skin—

rain and shale,
prickle-bite
of eucalyptus

a cold new creek
out there
somewhere

CAESAR AT SEVEN MONTHS

The third collar's
still stiff. He's climbed
through them, larger
and larger, like circus hoops.

Somewhere he bowed
to growing up, cocked
an ear to the song
of delicate manners.
Now there are other
cats in the world.

Where did he learn this gravity?
He slipped from the bottle
the genie brought him in
and can't get back,
marooned in the open
with his clear, new voice.

HOW INIKI GOT HER NAME

Recall the boats,
pray the wooden windows hold,
and bring the children in.
The chores have stopped,
the doors are locked,
and you wait
for the shrill old girl:
iniki, piercing wind.

She lies curled
off the coast,
feral stripes coiled
around the eye
of yin and yang,
due to blow ashore
at midnight.

Come morning,
your world will be cleared
of all you cared for,
save those you held
all through the howling.
Cane fields flat,
beaches torn
from their moorings,
green canyons
stripped to gray and brown,
the trail she left
of leaves on the sea,
your listing house
uncertain now,

trees piled like matches
on the lanai:
This she left you.

The cat sniffs gently
at raw edges
of rubble,
an ocean of new surfaces
snapped off, scraped clean,
exuding secret
inner scents.

ELEGY FOR TARA

Friends, I will spare you any report
of her love of milk. Enough to say
she was like and unlike every cat,
a small dame in a blue-fur ruff,
delicate as a dancer crossing
a room. And in her age
she let the world live on without her,
warm in the fold of a chair,
recording her days in doors opened
and closed, only deigning
to step outside if the weather
was gracious or the dark snap
of deer recalled her mousing past.
Everything must have looked larger
at the end. Still, she filled
her small space completely,
wise to the undulant skunks
and watching the doves like so many
miracles overhead.

SUNDAY

The cat doesn't talk commitment.
He's stretched out on my chest
like he's laid out at the beach,
kneading my shirt,
purring to himself.
If he knows the word *forever*,
it's locked in the matrix of his mouth,
reverberating his warm walls
of language. Likewise, *love*
never comes stumbling out
on a still Sunday morning,
his paws in my hair,
his breath in my ear
a sonnet.

STRAY

She was in the greenhouse,
curled, sleeping against
the rain pelting the glass wall.
She had no tag.
That I could see, her black neck
was bare, in fact
no spot anywhere on her,
this cat all black
without an errant hair.

I crept through the door,
and with the ears of a beggar
she heard me there.
She was sleek and frightened
and slick as oil under the flatbed,
sliding backward to a corner.
I reached a finger into the dark.
She purred, took a step, waited.
My finger found her ear,
soft as a bird,
and she bit—
a savage, sudden grab.

Outside the greenhouse,
blood ran in the rain
off my wrist, a gray knob
rose on my palm. *I never learn*, I shouted
(not to offer my hand,
just stood there convincing her
she needed help,
she needed me).

MIDDLE NAME

I decided the cat needed a middle name
as I waited for the vet to finish
pumping him full of fluids. Illness had made
this new cat mine. The way he'd struggled in the car,
claws snared in the bars of the cage,
dragged me back to three friends gone this winter.
He was too young for this.
And when he came home, tender from needle pricks,
high on the raw sugars of danger, he rubbed his face
on a chair leg, asked for food. You see, then,
I had to name this person
back from the dead—this April, Lazarus, love.

CAESAR AT 14 YEARS

Through the dark glass
of the back door,
I can't see
if he's still there.

Outside, the quiet tick
of rain. Lately he's taken
to a grove
of thick bamboo,
the cancer grown too wide
for him to lie
on bare earth, hard stone.

With the night's breath,
the curtain
waves open,
waves closed.

I see him now
under the patio's shelter,
his sharp spine
a soft orange brush,
his ears tracking
every small sound.

HIS BONES

shone through
the last
          few weeks
          sweet
   scaffolding

sharp
   like sandstone
      new   cut

how
   did they

      connect

long curve
               to
small
          heart
                    chamber

how
   did they cool
   in shade of skin

                         move
like hands
under a sheet

sharp
      tents
of knuckle
      and intent

our bones
                   called
    to
        each other

      called
      stay   just
      stay

AFTER

The rain left mirrors
on the flagstones
and the mayonnaise jar
upside down over last year's
dahlia stem made
a small new dish
that the cat lapped from,
one paw held up
out of the mud.

CAT, 3 A.M.

I am far
out at sea, adrift
on a dark mirror.
He calls from the continent
of waking, tolls
a lonely bell. The current
pulls me closer and he grabs
for the lines, catches my hair,
elbow, hand. It's a slow business,
but finally I'm aground.
Lights blink on—
bathroom, hall—the shore's
alive. And though
I've brought nothing he needs—
he had water, he had food—
still, he is glad for the company
and spins a small dance
in the kitchen cabana,
telling me a story
in the singing language
of his people.

Raised in northern California and western Massachusetts, Amy Miller worked as a horse wrangler, electronic assembler, photographer's assistant, and ad salesperson before settling into a career as an editor and print project manager. Her writing has appeared in *Northwest Review*, *Nimrod*, *Rattle*, *Many Mountains Moving*, *ZYZZYVA*, *Fine Gardening*, *The Writer's Journal*, *Tiny Lights*, and *The Poet's Market*, and anthologies such as *What the River Brings: Oregon River Poems* and *London Calling: A Clash Anthology*. She has won the *Whiskey Island* Poetry Prize, the Cultural Center of Cape Cod National Poetry Competition, and the *Cloudbank* Award, was a finalist in *A Prairie Home Companion's* Sonnet Contest and for the Pablo Neruda Prize and 49th Parallel Award, and has twice been nominated for the Pushcart prize. Her chapbooks of poetry and nonfiction include *Tea Before Questions*, *The Mechanics of the Rescue*, and *Fred Meyer, Mi Amore*. She currently works as the publications manager for the Oregon Shakespeare Festival and blogs at writers-island.blogspot.com.

www.ingramcontent.com/pod-product-compliance
Lightning Source LLC
Chambersburg PA
CBHW020956030426
42339CB00005B/134